# i-SPY

# countryside challenge

# DO IT! SCORE IT!

Published by Collins
An imprint of HarperCollins Publishers
Westerhill Road, Bishopbriggs, Glasgow G64 2QT
www.harpercollins.co.uk

HarperCollins Publishers
Macken House, 39/40 Mayor Street Upper, Dublin 1, D01 C9W8, Ireland

© Michelin Editions 2023
© HarperCollins Publishers 2023

A catalogue record for this book is available from the British Library.

ISBN 9780008562625

Printed in the UAE

10 9 8 7 6 5 4 3 2 1

Text by Heather Ryce
Front cover image © Sandra Standbridge/Shutterstock.com
All internal images © Shutterstock.com except pages 56 and 58 courtesy of
Jennifer Smith and Oliver Smith.

# i-SPY

# countryside challenge

## DO IT! SCORE IT!

# Contents

**Tick off each activity as you do it!**

# How to use this book

## Get ready to take on the i-SPY challenge with 50 activities to get closer to nature!

Once you've done each activity tick it off on the contents list. You can do them in any order you like.

Note to grown-up: Join in the fun by doing the activities together and supervise any that you feel necessary.

Look out for activities which have eco points. These are awarded for doing something that helps look after the planet and its wildlife. Once you score 200 eco points, send off for your i-SPY eco-hero certificate and badge.

As well as activities, the book is packed with facts, photos and things to spot. If you spy it, score it by ticking the circle or star. Items with a star are difficult to spot so you'll have to search high and low to find them. Once you score 1000 spotter points, send off for your i-SPY super-spotter certificate and badge.

## How to get your i-SPY certificates and badges

✓ Ask a grown-up to check your score.

✓ Apply for your certificate and badge at collins.co.uk/i-SPY (if you are under the age of 13 you'll need a parent or guardian to do this).

✓ We'll send you your certificate and badge!

# Walk in the countryside

The countryside has lots of natural features and is away from busy towns and cities. It is the perfect place to find peace and calm and connect with nature.

## You'll need: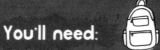

walking boots or sturdy shoes, layers of clothing, waterproofs/hat/scarf, packed lunch and water

## What to do:

**1** With an adult, plan a visit to countryside near you.

**2** Wear sturdy walking shoes and layers of clothing. Depending on the time of year, take waterproofs and a hat and scarf.

**3** Bring a packed lunch and remember to take lots of water to keep you hydrated.

**4** Breathe in the fresh air of the countryside, clear your mind of any worries and enjoy the spectacular views.

Walking keeps our bodies and minds healthy. You will always discover something new in the countryside, such as a bird you have never seen before, a secret path or an unusual tree species.

When you are in the countryside, can you spot these things?

Tractor
10 POINTS

Sheep
5 POINTS

Stream
15 POINTS

Hedgerow
10 POINTS

Stile
15 POINTS

Locked gate
10 POINTS

# Play walking bingo

Walking bingo is a great way to notice things when you are going for a walk in the countryside. It is lots of fun to play with other people, but you can do the activity on your own too.

## You'll need:

this book, pencil

## What to do:

**1** Look at the things to spot on the next page, so you know what you need to look out for on your walk. If an adult is not playing the game with you, always let them know where you will be going.

**2** Try to find all the spots on your walk. If you are playing the game with other people, try to find them all first! Use a pencil to tick off each spot as you come across it.

**3** When you have found all the spots, shout 'Bingo!'.

**4** You can find the spots more than once when you go out for a walk in the countryside. Or you could make up some spots of your own.

Remember to tick off the spots and yell 'Bingo!' when you have found them all.

A dog barking
○ **10** POINTS

Someone wearing a hat
○ **10** POINTS

A squirrel
○ **10** POINTS

Something yellow
○ **10** POINTS

A flying insect
○ **10** POINTS

A pine cone
○ **10** POINTS

A puddle
○ **10** POINTS

A bird of prey
○ **10** POINTS

# Take a photo of every season

Why do we have seasons? The Earth journeys around the sun in a tilted position. The angle of the tilt affects the amount of daylight each hemisphere gets, which leads to hotter or colder temperatures.

Each season in the UK is known for different things, such as flowers blooming in spring, warm nights in summer, leaves falling in autumn and snow in winter. Capturing these moments in a photograph allows you to see how an area changes depending on the season.

## You'll need:

camera

## What to do:

**1** Choose a favourite place in the countryside.

**2** Take a photo of the place every three months. Capture as much of the landscape and sky as you can.

**3** How does the place change in your photos every season?

**4** Print out your photos and put them in a scrapbook. Fill your scrapbook by going back to your favourite place each year and seeing the changes over a long period of time.

Can you spot these signs of the different seasons in the countryside?

## Red sky at night

**15** POINTS

## Pile of fallen leaves

**5** POINTS

## Daffodils growing

**10** POINTS

## Young animal

**25** POINTS

## Snow

**15** POINTS

## Frozen river

**15** POINTS

13

# Cook outside

If you have spent the day exploring the countryside, why not cook and eat dinner outside too?

There are different ways to prepare food outside, including a barbecue grill, pizza oven, campfire grate and tripod cooking pot.

## You'll need:

prepared food, camping stove, cutlery and cooking equipment, napkins

## What to do:

**1** Before you leave for your day out, prepare as much food as possible. For example, wash and chop vegetables, and cook food to reheat later. Also organise the cooking equipment and cutlery that you will need. It may be useful to write a list, so you don't forget something essential.

**2** With the help of an adult, test your camping stove before you set off.

**3** After you have eaten outside, make sure you take home all of your equipment and rubbish. Leave no trace that you were in the countryside.

Score 30 eco points for being part of the Leave No Trace scheme. Find out more on their website.

**30** ECO POINTS

When you are cooking outside, can you spot these things?

Smoke
5 POINTS

Tongs
5 POINTS

Fallen-over log
5 POINTS

Fire
5 POINTS

Ketchup
5 POINTS

Rubbish bin
5 POINTS

15

# Forage for berries

From summer to autumn, you can forage (search) for berries. Berries grow in many places, but you will often find them in hedgerows. You can make berries into pies, syrups and jams, or just have a healthy snack on the go.

Some berries can make you sick, so always check with an adult before eating anything you have collected. Only eat a berry if you are sure you know what it is. It's useful to research what kinds of berries are safe to eat before picking your own.

## You'll need:

basket or bowl

## What to do:

**1** Use your basket or bowl to collect and store your berries.

**2** Take only what you intend to eat. Wildlife love to snack on berries too, so don't let any go to waste.

**3** Only collect berries where there are lots growing in the area. Always stick to paths when picking them, so that you don't damage the environment around you.

**4** Wash your berries with cold water before eating them.

Try to spot these berries, which you can safely eat when out and about.

Blackberries
**10** POINTS

Raspberries
**10** POINTS

Bilberries
**15** POINTS

Rowan berries
**15** POINTS

Gooseberries
**15** POINTS

Sea buckthorn

TOP SPOT!

**40** POINTS

# Make jam

With time and patience, you can make your own jam.

Jam is made from pieces of fruit. The fruit is usually cooked with sugar and crushed, so the pectin (component found in the cells of plants) releases and the mixture thickens until it is a jam-like consistency.

## You'll need:

4 cups of fresh berries, 1 cup of sugar, 3 tablespoons of pectin powder, blender, spoons, pot, jam jars

## What to do:

**1** With the help of an adult, blend your berries until they are a thick mush. Use your spoon to press the mixture if it is too lumpy.

**2** Pour your crushed berries into a pot. Then add sugar and pectin powder. Carefully cook your mixture over a medium heat until it begins to bubble.

**3** Boil the jam for five more minutes, stirring regularly.

**4** Pour the jam into jam jars and leave it to cool for a few hours.

**5** Store the jam for up to two weeks in the fridge.

Score 30 eco points for making jam from berries you have foraged.

**30** ECO POINTS

# Find out what way the wind is blowing

Knowing what way the wind is blowing can be useful for all sorts of reasons. Remember, the wind direction is always determined by where the wind is blowing from, not where it is blowing towards.

## You'll need:

compass, bowl of water

## What to do:

**1** The countryside is an ideal place to find out what way the wind is blowing as there are many areas of open, flat land.

**2** First, using a compass, find out the direction you are facing so that you can work out the direction of the wind.

**3** Next, wet your index finger by dipping it into a bowl of water. Then point it upwards away from your body.

**4** The side of your finger that feels cool from the wind is the direction it is blowing from.

**5** If you are finding it hard to work out what way the wind is blowing, close your eyes and concentrate only on the sensation of your finger.

# Help with lambing

Lambing takes place on British farms between November and May, but most ewes give birth in spring after a gestation period (the time it takes for the lamb to grow inside its mum) of around five months.

Lambing season is a busy time on a farm and farmers often look for volunteers to help them.

## You'll need:

internet access, help from an adult

## What to do:

**1** With the help of an adult, look on the internet and find local farms in need of volunteers. Alternatively, book a lambing experience where you can watch lambs being born, bottle-feed them and help keep them clean and warm.

**2** If you are not old enough to be able to help with lambing, visit a farm or an animal park where you can see lambs up close and ask questions about lambing.

See if you can spot these things during lambing season.

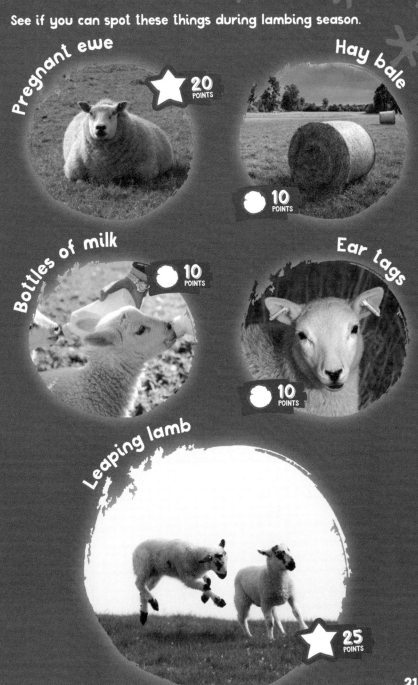

**Pregnant ewe**
20 POINTS

**Hay bale**
10 POINTS

**Bottles of milk**
10 POINTS

**Ear tags**
10 POINTS

**Leaping lamb**
25 POINTS

# Visit a waterfall

Waterfalls form when rivers flow over soft rock, which leads to vertical erosion of the ground. There are many waterfalls around the UK to visit and it can be fun to compare their heights, location and flow of water.

## You'll need:

sturdy boots, camera

## What to do:

**1** With the help of an adult, research waterfalls to visit. Here are some ideas.

The Grey Mare's Tail waterfall in Dumfries is one of the tallest waterfalls in Britain. At certain times of year it is covered in vibrant purple heather.

Pistyll Rhaeadr waterfall in Powys, is steep. It is framed beautifully in greenery.

Gaping Gill waterfall in North Yorkshire is unique because the water pours underground. If you visit the waterfall, you will also find the cave entrance. It is an unforgettable sight!

**2** How many waterfalls can you visit in a year?

When you are visiting a waterfall, look around and see if you can spot...

Fast-flowing water
**5** POINTS

Plunge pool
**15** POINTS

Hydroelectric plant

TOP SPOT!

**40** POINTS

Rainbow
**20** POINTS

Bridge
**10** POINTS

Algae on rocks
**10** POINTS

23

# Go for a wild swim

Wild swimming can be really good for you. The cold water can help with muscle aches, improve circulation and has been shown to boost the immune system too.

## You'll need:

internet access, swimming costume, appropriate shoes, towel, layers of clothes

## What to do:

**1** With the help of an adult, find areas suitable for wild swimming around the UK.

**2** Before you go for a dip, make sure you are warmed up. Plan a brisk walk to the river and wear layers of clothes.

**3** Check carefully for signs telling you not to swim at that location and never go swimming without adult supervision.

**4** Before you get into the water, find an area where it is easy to get back out and only proceed if the weather and water are calm. When you first get in, it will feel cold, but keep going for a few minutes and your body will adapt.

When you are wild swimming, avoid contact with blue-green algae, cover any cuts with waterproof plasters before swimming and never jump into the water without checking how deep it is.

Can you spot this wildlife when you are wild swimming?

Stickleback
**15** POINTS

Kingfisher
**25** POINTS

Brown trout
**15** POINTS

Freshwater eel
**15** POINTS

Beaver

TOP SPOT!

**40** POINTS

# Go fishing

Fishing takes patience but is a rewarding activity. You may need to apply for a rod licence. Ask an adult about this. Also make sure it isn't 'close season', which means you cannot fish.

## You'll need:

internet access, rod licence, fishing rod, barbless hooks, sun cream

## What to do:

**1** Research online where the best places to fish are near you.

**2** Plan your day. Consider the weather, take plenty of food and water, and wear sun cream if it is warm outside.

**3** Ask an adult to help you choose a fishing rod — you can rent or buy rods depending on how often you want to fish.

**4** Using barbless hooks means you can return fish back to the river unharmed. Don't pull on the line to remove the hook; always take the time to remove it properly. Never throw fish back into the water. Gently lower them to the surface and allow them to swim away from your hands.

Score 30 eco points for returning fish you have caught unharmed.

**30**
ECO POINTS

When you're fishing, which of these fish can you spot?

Minnow

**10** POINTS

Perch

**15** POINTS

Common carp

**15** POINTS

Bream

**15** POINTS

Pike

**30** POINTS

River lamprey

TOP SPOT!

**40** POINTS

# Go kayaking or canoeing

Kayaking and canoeing are fun to do and they are excellent forms of exercise.

You can join a club or hire equipment for a few hours to explore some amazing open water spots around the UK. Always carry out this activity under the supervision of an adult and never enter the water alone.

## You'll need:

lifejacket, paddle, hat

## What to do:

**1** Choose a calm body of water on a sunny day with a gently sloping area of land to launch.

**2** Test out your kayak or canoe on land and get used to how it will feel in the water.

**3** Sit upright to make it easier to keep your balance and be able to paddle.

**4** Your knees should be slightly bent when sitting in the kayak/canoe. You should fit snugly, but with enough room to manoeuvre if you capsize.

**5** When entering the water, hold the paddle with both hands in the centre. Keep your elbows bent as you paddle using a forward stroke.

Along the river, can you spot...?

Lifejacket

5 POINTS

Paddle

5 POINTS

Lifebuoy

15 POINTS

Reflection in the water
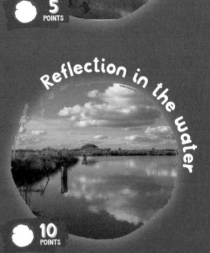
10 POINTS

Swan

10 POINTS

Coot

15 POINTS

# Find a bird's nest

Finding a bird's nest can be tricky, but there are a few tips you can follow.

Never touch a nest with eggs or fledglings inside, as this could lead to adult birds abandoning their young. It is also illegal to disturb the nests and eggs of some protected species of bird. Visit the RSPB website for more information.

## You'll need:

binoculars, map, pen

## What to do:

**1** Look out for nests in winter: you will spot nests more easily when leaves have fallen.

**2** Listen for birds during the breeding season. Mark their location on a map as this area could indicate where they have built their nest.

**3** Use binoculars to track birds early in spring when they may be carrying material to build their nest.

**4** When you find a nest, always keep your distance so you don't scare birds away or damage the nest site.

Can you spot these bird nests?

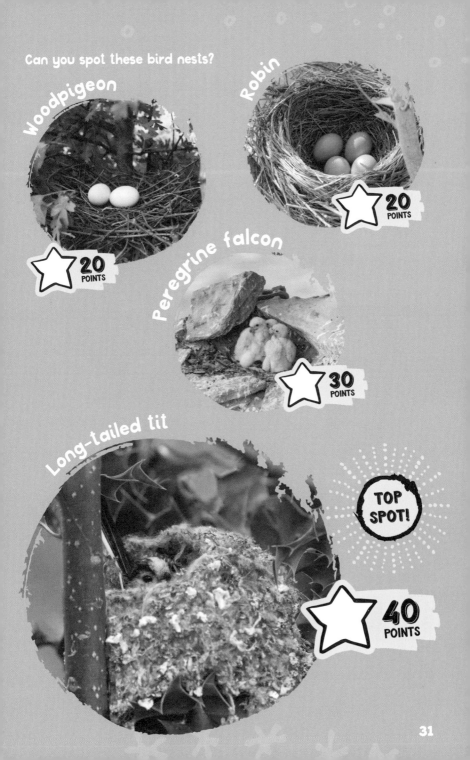

Woodpigeon

Robin

20 POINTS

20 POINTS

Peregrine falcon

30 POINTS

Long-tailed tit

TOP SPOT!

40 POINTS

# Make a tyre swing

You can make a tyre swing in the countryside if you return the area to how you found it and cause no damage to the tree. It's a fun outdoor activity, but be careful and always ask permission from an adult.

## You'll need:

upcycled tyre, heavy duty rope

## What to do:

**1** Choose a tree for your tyre swing. The tree should be large and healthy with a branch at least 20 cm thick. Double check the tree you have chosen isn't protected in any way – if in doubt, contact your local authority for more information.

**2** Clear the area under the branch of your tree of any rocks or hazards. Make sure there is enough clearance between where the tyre hangs and the trunk of the tree, as well as the ground.

**3** Upcycle an old tyre (such as a car tyre) to use as a swing. You may wish to clean the tyre before attaching it to the tree.

**4** Cut a section of rope to the required length (including extra to make knots). With the help of an adult, tie a double bowline knot on one end of the rope, leaving a little slack in the loop of the knot.

**5** Throw the knot end of the rope over the branch and thread the opposite end through the loop of the bowline knot. Pull tight.

**6** Tie another bowline knot around the tyre. Pull tight so it is secure and the tyre suspends at the desired height.

**7** Test the swing under the supervision of an adult, by sitting still in the tyre. When you are confident it holds your weight, swing away!

Score 20 eco points for removing your swing once you have finished and taking your materials home with you.

**20** ECO POINTS

# Spot a red squirrel

Spotting a red squirrel for the first time is unforgettable. Sadly, the introduction of the North American grey squirrel to the UK has caused the numbers of red squirrels to decline.

## You'll need:

internet access, camera, binoculars, warm clothing

## What to do:

**1** Autumn is the best time to look for red squirrels, as they spend time on the ground finding nuts for the cold winter months.

**2** Research where your best chance is to see a red squirrel near you. You may have to travel to a nature reserve, like Smardale Gill in Cumbria. Visit The Wildlife Trusts website for more information on red squirrel sites in the UK.

**3** Look for signs that a red squirrel could be close by, such as a nibbled pine cone, or use your binoculars to spot a drey (a squirrel's home). Red squirrels like to build their dreys high in the canopy in the fork of a tree branch.

**4** If you're lucky enough to see a red squirrel, take a picture, but remember to turn off the flash.

When you're visiting areas where red squirrels live, how many of these things can you spot?

**Drey** 25 POINTS

**Nibbled pine cone** 15 POINTS

**Coniferous woodland** 15 POINTS

**Squirrel crossing sign** CAUTION Red squirrels crossing 15 POINTS

**Red squirrel** TOP SPOT! 40 POINTS

Score 40 eco points for supporting red squirrel conservation projects and visiting squirrel habitats.

40 ECO POINTS

# Identify the poo!

It can be difficult to work out where to see some animals and waiting for them to appear can take a long time. However, many animals leave clues behind such as poo. If you can identify the poo, it may be easier to track down the animal you wish to see.

Some poo can be identified quickly, but sometimes it needs a closer look!

## You'll need:

camera, gloves, clear jar, hand sanitiser

## What to do:

**1** Use the next page to identify animal poo you come across in the countryside. Or take a photo of the poo and do research when you get home.

**2** If you come across poo which you cannot identify easily, use gloves to put it into a clear jar so that you can look at it more closely.

**3** If the poo has pieces of bone or fur in it, it may belong to an animal that eats other animals. If the poo is round and dry, it may belong to wildlife that eats grass.

**4** Always wash your hands thoroughly after touching animal poo.

# Can you spot the animal poo?!

**15 POINTS**

Fox poo is easy to spot on paths. It is similar to dog poo, but with a pointy end and musky smell. You may find fur, feathers, bone and berries inside.

**35 POINTS**

Hedgehog poo is long and cylindrical. It is dark in colour with patches of shiny insect remains. This poo has an unpleasant smell.

**15 POINTS**

Roe deer poo is found in small piles along paths or in fields. It is ball-like in shape with a shine to it.

**10 POINTS**

Rabbit poo is dry and pea-sized. It is found in piles in grass and crumbles when broken up by hand. You sometimes find grass or hair inside the poo (from when the rabbits groom themselves).

# Look for owl pellets

Animal poo isn't the only way to learn about the wildlife around you – there are other clues such as regurgitated food. Owl pellets are the regurgitated parts of the bird's food that it could not digest, such as hair and bone. As many owls swallow their prey whole, you may find skulls of prey like mice and voles in a pellet.

## You'll need:

gloves, clear jar/tupperware, hand sanitiser

## What to do:

**1** First, find out where owls live locally. Listen for them calling or ask a local bird-watching group where to find them. Many owls go hunting at night, eat what they catch and then sit nearby in a tree.

**2** You are searching for a dark-coloured pellet 2–5 cm long. They are usually found around the base of large trees or at entrances to barns/stables.

**3** Bring gloves and a jar/tupperware so that you can examine the pellet closely. Can you identify what prey the owl has caught from the bones that have been regurgitated?

**4** Always wash your hands after touching a pellet.

While you're looking for owl pellets, see if you can spot these owl species.

Tawny owl

⭐ **20** POINTS

Little owl

⭐ **20** POINTS

Barn owl

⭐ **20** POINTS

Long-eared owl

⭐ **30** POINTS

Short-eared owl

⭐ **35** POINTS

# Track an animal

You don't need to stay inside on rainy or snowy days: brave the raindrops and snow to track down wildlife! When soft ground becomes soaked or covered, tracks are left behind. Use your observational skills to locate tracks and identify which animal has been in the area.

Tracks offer clues that let us know what animals are around, where they are travelling and if they are moving in groups or on their own. This is all useful information for budding animal detectives!

## You'll need:

notepad and pen,
raincoat or winter coat/
hat/scarf

## What to do:

**1** When it is still wet or there is snow, search the ground for animal tracks.

**2** In a notepad, write down the tracks you see. You could also sketch them to help you remember and compare them with other tracks.

**3** Can you identify the species from the track and tell in what direction the animal is moving?

Can you spot these animal tracks?

### Pawprint

If the track is a pawprint shape with four toes, it is likely to be from a mammal like a dog, cat or fox.

**20 POINTS**

### Hoofprint

If the track has two long teardrop shapes, it will probably have been made by a deer.

**15 POINTS**

### Bird track

If the track is made of three or four lines or narrow points, it's a good sign that a bird was in the area.

**15 POINTS**

### Horse track

**15 POINTS**

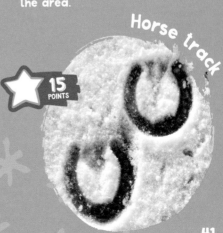

It should be fairly easy to spot the track of a horse from its striking horseshoe shape.

# Visit a nature reserve

Nature reserves are wonderful places to see the natural world undisturbed by human activity. Reserves can range from protected meadows to wetlands, mountains and ancient woodland. Their purpose is to allow plants and animals to thrive and to provide an outdoor space for people to connect with nature.

There are hundreds of nature reserves in the UK – how many can you visit?

## You'll need:

map, internet access

## What to do:

**1** Search the internet for nature reserves, either by distance from where you live or by the animals/plants you want to see. Websites like the RSPB, National Trust and The Wildlife Trusts have lists and details of nature reserves, so they are a great source of information to begin your search.

**2** With the help of an adult, plan where you would like to visit. You could make a top ten list and try to visit them all in a year!

Score 20 eco points for visiting a nature reserve and finding out about the plants and animals that live there.

**20 ECO POINTS**

# Write a letter to protect the countryside

Not every part of the countryside is a nature reserve. If you come across a green space that has been damaged, or disagree with government plans to build houses or other developments in a countryside area, write a letter to your MP (Member of Parliament).

## You'll need:

internet access, paper, envelope, pen

## What to do:

**1** Ask an adult to help you find out who your local MP is. When you know their name, you will be able to find out the best way to contact them.

**2** Begin your letter or email by outlining the environmental issue and where exactly in the countryside the problem is.

**3** State why you disagree with the changes to the area and what you would like to happen instead. Keep your letter polite and informative.

**4** Leave your name, age and contact details at the end of the letter, so your MP can reply with the actions they have taken in response to your concerns.

# Collect rubbish from hedgerows

Rubbish looks horrible but is also harmful to wildlife and pollutes the environment. When rubbish is caught in the wind, it can be blown across the landscape and collect in places like hedgerows.

Hedgerows are homes to many insects and birds. They are a vital food source and animals like harvest mice travel through them.

Why not help the countryside by clearing the hedgerows?

## You'll need:

gloves, binbags, camera

## What to do:

**1** Ask permission from an adult before you collect rubbish. Always work in a safe area away from main roads.

**2** Take a 'before' photo and then get to work clearing as much rubbish as you can. Sort the rubbish for recycling.

**3** How many bags of rubbish did you fill? Once you have finished, take an 'after' photo and ask an adult to share your hard work with friends and family.

Score 30 eco points for helping wildlife by removing rubbish from their habitats.

**30**
ECO
POINTS

When you are clearing hedgerows, can you spot...?

Blue tit
5 POINTS

Bullfinch
15 POINTS

Whitethroat
20 POINTS

Goat moth
35 POINTS

Bank vole
30 POINTS

Common lizard
35 POINTS

# Build a den

Building a den is a fun activity to do with family or friends. Autumn is the best time for den building because it's easier to find branches and leaves that have fallen from trees.

Be considerate when you are building a den — try not to disturb the animals and plants that live in some parts of ancient woodland.

## You'll need:

branches, long sticks, thin sticks and twigs, dry leaves, foliage

## What to do:

**1** Look for leaves, branches and sticks. Don't break off branches from trees or use bracken, which can contain ticks (small, spider-like creatures that can spread disease to people).

**2** Look for a tree with a low branch.

**3** Line up the long sticks on each side of the branch to create a triangle shape.

**4** Fill in any gaps with the smaller, thin sticks and twigs to give the den a solid structure.

**5** Add foliage and leaves to the outside of the den.

**6** Take your den down when you have finished playing. Next time, you can try a different design!

# Write about your day out

A day out in the countryside can be a wonderful memory. Reflecting on your day means you can revisit your memories whenever you want.

## You'll need:

scrapbook and pens, items from your day out, sticky tape or glue, stickers

## What to do:

**1** When you are in the countryside, keep an eye out for items that remind you of your day. For example, a pretty leaf or a feather you discover on the ground.

**2** Write about your day in a scrapbook as soon as you return home. Include as much detail as you can. What did you see? What was your favourite part? How did you feel and what did you learn from your day?

**3** Decorate your scrapbook entry with your collected items, sketches and stickers.

**4** Write about all your favourite days out and build up a scrapbook of memories that you can visit any time you want.

Score 20 eco points for using a scrapbook made from recycled materials.

**20** ECO POINTS

# Cycle through the countryside

Cycling is lots of fun and great exercise.

## You'll need:

bike, helmet

## What to do:

**1** Organise a group bike ride or plan a route with an adult.

**2** Always remember to wear a helmet when cycling, and check the brakes and gears are working on your bike before you leave.

**3** Pack plenty of water to keep you hydrated throughout the day.

**4** When you are in the countryside, keep to unobstructed, marked paths. If you come across a blocked path, such as from a fallen tree, report this on your local council's website.

**5** Always give passers-by plenty of notice and room to move out of your way or manoeuvre around you. Slow right down or come to a complete stop when passing horses or livestock.

**6** If you are passing through closed gates, always close them again behind you.

**7** Have fun feeling the wind on your face and exploring a new route on a bike!

When you're cycling, can you spot...?

Other cyclists — **5** POINTS

Ferns — **10** POINTS

Woodland — **15** POINTS

Bench — **15** POINTS

Signpost — **10** POINTS

Horses — **20** POINTS

49

# Discover ancient woodlands

Ancient woodlands have been around from 1600 in England and Wales, and 1750 in Scotland. They cover less than 3% of the UK. Ancient woodlands have communities of animals and plants not found anywhere else; they also have important archaeological features.

These special places are under threat from overgrazing, human activity and the spread of invasive species such as rhododendron.

## You'll need:

internet access, camera, notebook, pen

## What to do:

**1** Most ancient woodlands have been discovered and mapped, so you can easily find locations near you with a quick internet search. Ask an adult to help you.

**2** When you have chosen a site to visit, remember to pack a camera and a notebook so that you can write about your time in the woodland. Note how standing in such a historical place makes you feel.

**3** Sign up to organisations such as The Woodland Trust to find out more about ancient woodlands.

Some species are ancient woodland indicators – the more of these species you spot, the more likely it is that the area you are in is ancient.

**Bluebells**
⭐ **15** POINTS

**Wood anemone**
⭐ **20** POINTS

**Wild service tree**
⭐ **25** POINTS

**Lemon slug**
⭐ **30** POINTS

**Violet click beetle**
⭐ **35** POINTS

Score 30 eco points for finding out more about how you can help protect ancient woodlands.

**30** ECO POINTS

# Take a bark rubbing

The bark of a tree is, in many ways, similar to our skin, because it is essential for a tree's survival. Bark keeps in moisture, fights infection and transfers vital sugars up and down the tree. Many animals use it to make homes and some insects feed on it.

Bark can be rough, smooth, hard or soft depending on the health and species of tree. Why not take a closer look?

## You'll need:

paper, crayons

## What to do:

**1** Next time you know you are going to be around different types of trees, pack some paper and crayons.

**2** Choose the tree you would like to take a rubbing from. Then put a piece of paper on top of a section of bark.

**3** With one hand, hold the paper firmly to the tree. Use the other to rub a crayon gently over the paper.

**4** When you have coloured in the paper, remove it and take a closer look. How does the bark rubbing compare to other species of tree?

You can identify a tree species from its leaves but also its bark. How many of these different kinds of bark can you spot?

Silver birch **15** POINTS

Aspen **15** POINTS

Sycamore **15** POINTS

Ash **15** POINTS

Beech **20** POINTS

Scotch pine **20** POINTS

Cherry **25** POINTS

Oak **15** POINTS

# Go geocaching

Geocaching is a fun activity to do with family and friends. It uses GPS (Global Positioning System) coordinates to help you find a series of caches, or prizes.

## You'll need:

internet access, handheld GPS navigation device or smartphone with GPS connectivity, backpack, walking boots, cache prize

## What to do:

1. With the help of an adult, sign up for a free account on the geocaching website and download the app to a smartphone. You will then be able to map where the caches are in your area.

2. When you are geocaching, wear comfortable clothes and walking boots.

3. The cache container may be tricky to find, for example, hidden behind a log. Keep your eyes peeled!

4. When you have located the cache, record your details in the logbook and take your prize.

5. Leave a prize in the cache container for the next person to find. Never leave valuable items or food in the container.

6. Share your find on the app and how quickly or easily you located the cache.

Sometimes people come across unusual finds in a cache, but here are some common items to spot.

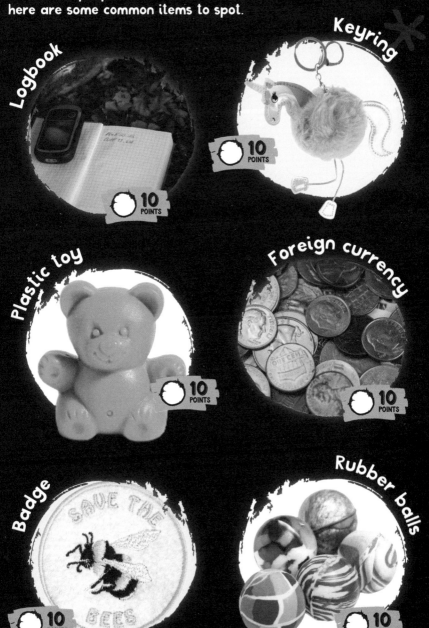

Logbook
**10** POINTS

Keyring
**10** POINTS

Plastic toy
**10** POINTS

Foreign currency
**10** POINTS

Badge
SAVE THE BEES
**10** POINTS

Rubber balls
**10** POINTS

# Make an autumn wreath

An autumn wreath can add a unique touch to your home or make a great gift for a family member or friend.

## You'll need:

large paper plate, items such as leaves, twigs, pine cones, glue, scissors, ribbon or string

## What to do:

1. When you are out for a walk in autumn, collect natural items you would like to include in your wreath. For example, different-coloured leaves, conkers, twigs and pine cones.

2. Bring the items home and lay them in front of you on a table so you can see everything that you have collected.

3. Make a small hole at the top of your paper plate so that you can hang the wreath later. Then, with the help of an adult, cut out the middle of your plate so you are left with a doughnut shape.

4. Begin to decorate your wreath. Glue the larger items down first.

5. When you have finished, thread the ribbon or string through the hole and welcome in autumn with your hanging wreath.

# Kick up some leaves

In autumn, the production of a hormone called auxin reduces in some trees. This causes the bond between leaf and branch to weaken until eventually the leaf falls off. Why? If a tree gets rid of its leaves in autumn, it saves precious energy through the cold, harsh months of winter.

There are many activities and crafts to do with fallen leaves, but one simple, joyful activity is leaf kicking. Go on, give it a go!

## You'll need:

sturdy shoes or boots, pile of leaves

## What to do:

**1** On a dry day, find an area in the countryside where there are piles of fallen leaves.

**2** Kick the leaves high into the air! How high can you kick them? How many can you kick at once?

**3** Have competitions with friends to see who the best leaf kicker is.

Score 30 eco points for gathering leaves into a pile at the bottom of a tree for insects to make a home or for hibernating amphibians.

**30** ECO POINTS

# Make a scarecrow

The purpose of scarecrows, as their name suggests, is to scare crows from vegetable patches and crops on farms.

## You'll need:

old broom, old T-shirt, straw, duct tape, coloured markers, glue, small plant pot, old hat

## What to do:

**1** Ask an adult to remove the head from an old broom.

**2** Stuff an old T-shirt with straw. Secure it at the bottom with duct tape so the stuffing doesn't fall out. Leave a small gap for the broom handle to go through.

**3** Put a small plant pot upside down. This will be your scarecrow's face. Draw a smiling face with permanent markers.

**4** With an adult's help, thread the broom handle through the bottom of the T-shirt and out through the neck. Secure the top of the broom in the upside-down pot with glue.

**5** Add a hat to your scarecrow and any other decorations.

**6** Ask an adult to wedge the bottom of the broom handle into the ground. This will keep your scarecrow upright in the wind while guarding your vegetable patch.

How many of these can you spot when you are in and around fields?

**Cow**

5 POINTS

**Scarecrow**

20 POINTS

**Raven**

10 POINTS

**Lapwing**

TOP SPOT!

40 POINTS

**Plough**

10 POINTS

**Barley**

15 POINTS

# Whistle with a piece of grass

Do you find it hard to whistle? Or are you still learning to whistle with two fingers?

If so, you can impress your friends by whistling in a different way. Next time you're outside, try whistling with a blade of grass and see how many people notice!

## You'll need:

blade of grass

## What to do:

**1** Choose a flat blade of grass that is at least as long as your thumb.

**2** Hold the grass lengthwise between your thumbs, pressing your knuckles together and with your fingernails facing you.

**3** Make sure the grass is pulled very tight between your thumbs.

**4** Purse your lips, put your mouth to your thumbs and blow. Don't worry if you don't make a sound the first time; just keep moving your thumbs slightly until you do.

**5** You can change the pitch of your whistle by cupping your hands.

# Dance in the rain

Wet weather shouldn't stop you from going outside and exploring the countryside. The secret is to embrace the rain and make the most of it.

## You'll need:

jacket, welly boots

## What to do:

**1** If you are outside and it begins to rain, try not to complain. Choose to dance instead! Splash in puddles, kick the water high into the air and wave your arms around! Enjoy being in the rain.

**2** Dancing in the rain can teach us to always look for the positive in challenging situations. It reminds us to be grateful even for the things we think of as an inconvenience – after all, without rain there would be no flowers or animals.

**3** When you have finished dancing outside, remember to take a hot shower or bath and dry off thoroughly.

# Make a nature mandala

Mandala is Sanskrit for circle. The circular design of a nature mandala is a symbol for the cycle of seasons, from spring, summer, autumn to winter and then back to spring again.

## You'll need:

bag/basket, scissors, camera, flat surface

## What to do:

**1** When you are in the countryside, collect items for your mandala in your bag/basket. Only take what you need. Try to find a few of the same thing if you want your mandala to look symmetrical.

**2** Sort your items onto a flat surface when you return home.

**3** Design your mandala outside or on a table or tray. Choose a centrepiece to start with and then make a pattern with the rest of the items, working out from the middle.

**4** Carry on until you have used up all your items. Then take a photo of your mandala.

**5** Create a nature mandala each season and compare how different they are.

For your nature mandala, can you find something...

that represents spring

**10** POINTS

**15** POINTS

that represents autumn

that smells nice

**10** POINTS

that's pointy

that's small

**10** POINTS

**10** POINTS

# 34

# Press flowers

Pressing flowers is a relaxing
activity. You can use pressed
flowers to decorate your
home or as gifts.

## You'll need:

basket or bag, flowers, heavy books, parchment paper

## What to do:

**1** When you are in the countryside, look for colourful, dry,
unblemished flowers that have a flat bud. This makes
them easier to press. Take only a small amount from
a single area.

**2** Bring your flowers home and prepare them by removing
any unwanted leaves.

**3** Open a large book (something like a dictionary) and put
pieces of parchment paper between the pages. A few
pages may get moisture on them from the flowers.

**4** Transfer your flowers to the open book and carefully
close it. Try not to move the flowers between the pages.

**5** Move your book to an area where it won't be opened.
Then put more heavy books on top of it.

**6** Leave the book closed for 3–4 weeks.

**7** Once the flowers are pressed, use them to add colour
to your home or as gifts for others.

Can you spot these flowers to press?

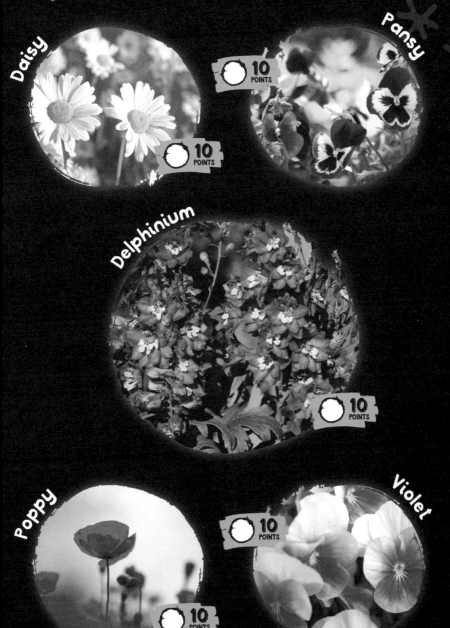

Daisy

**10** POINTS

Pansy

**10** POINTS

Delphinium

**10** POINTS

Poppy

**10** POINTS

Violet

**10** POINTS

# Make a daisy chain

Daisies are often found in the countryside, so it should be easy to find enough of them to make a simple daisy chain necklace or bracelet.

## You'll need:

basket, lots of daisies

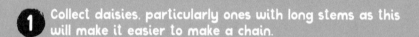

## What to do:

1. Collect daisies, particularly ones with long stems as this will make it easier to make a chain.

2. Once you have a small pile, take one daisy and pierce a small hole near the bottom of the stem with your fingernail.

3. Take another daisy and thread its stem through the hole.

4. Repeat the process by piercing a hole in the second daisy's stem and sliding a third flower through.

5. Continue doing this until you have a long chain. When you are happy with the length of the chain, thread your last daisy stem through the first daisy to make a loop.

In Norse mythology, the daisy was sacred and the flower of the goddess of love and beauty. It symbolised new beginnings. Remember this when you are wearing your daisy chain and channel that positivity!

# Do the buttercup test

One way to find out if someone likes butter is to hold a freshly picked buttercup under their chin. There may not be actual science to back this up, but it is fun to try!

## You'll need:

buttercup, friend or family member, mirror

## What to do:

**1** Pick a buttercup from a grassy field.

**2** Hold the buttercup under the chin of a friend or family member.

**3** If their chin glows yellow, they like butter! Try it on yourself too using a mirror.

Why do buttercups seem to shine yellow under your chin? Well, it's a flower's job to look colourful to attract pollinators such as butterflies and bees, but the glow from a buttercup is unique because no other plant reflects colour and light in the same way. The glowing effect is created by layers of air just below the surface of the petals that reflect light back and cause your chin to light up!

# Visit a wind farm

On a wind farm, many wind turbines are grouped together to use the power of the wind to generate electricity. The land may also be used for farming and is often located near water.

Visit a wind farm near you to learn more about this form of sustainable energy and spot wildlife like deer and birds of prey.

## You'll need:

warm clothing, bottle of water, camera, binoculars

## What to do:

**1** With an adult, find a wind farm you would like to visit.

**2** Wear warm clothing — wind farms are windy! Take water with you as wind farms often have long, scenic routes, and you need to stay hydrated.

**3** Take photos of the wind turbines. You should be able to see them up close and hear the 'whoosh' noise as they turn.

**4** Use binoculars to look more closely at the wildlife on the wind farm.

Score 40 eco points for finding out about the clean and renewable energy that wind farms create.

**40 ECO POINTS**

When walking around a wind farm, can you see...?

Wind turbine
10 POINTS

Cattle grid
10 POINTS

Body of water
15 POINTS

Roe deer
20 POINTS

Wheatear
30 POINTS

Hen harrier
TOP SPOT!
40 POINTS

# 38

# Go on a wild mushroom hunt

Did you know that mushrooms and toadstools are
neither animal nor plant, but their
own unique group of living
things called fungi.

Not all mushrooms in the
wild are safe to eat. Some
fungi are poisonous, so
never touch or pick them
without permission from an
adult.

## You'll need:

camera, notepad and pen

## What to do:

**1** Mushrooms grow everywhere from the ground to on trees.
Autumn is when they are happiest because of the cooler
temperatures and heavier rainfall, so that is the best
time to go on a hunt.

**2** Look at damp places like rotten tree stumps, as this is
where mushrooms tend to grow.

**3** Take a photo or sketch the mushrooms you find. Also write
down if they smell or have an unusual texture – this will
help you work out what kind of species you have found.

**4** As you explore, you'll start to learn where certain
mushrooms tend to grow and get quicker at finding them.

On your mushroom hunt, can you spot these common species?

Oyster mushroom
**10** POINTS

Chanterelle mushroom
**20** POINTS

Giant puffball
**25** POINTS

Jelly ear
**25** POINTS

Shaggy inkcap
**30** POINTS

Chicken of the woods
**35** POINTS

# 39

# Make elderflower cordial

Elderflowers are the edible blossoms of the elder tree, which is widespread across the UK.

Making elderflower cordial is a great activity to do in spring and the cordial tastes very refreshing. It's satisfying to enjoy something you made from scratch. Ask an adult to help you with this activity.

## You'll need:

basket, elderflowers, unwaxed lemons, citric acid, white sugar, two pots, tablecloth, sieve, glass bottles

## What to do:

**1** On a dry day in spring, pick a pile of elderflowers from an elder tree and put them in a basket. Pick at least 20 elderflowers to make a substantial amount of cordial. Avoid picking elderflowers from roadsides. Choose flowers that have fully opened, but not started to wilt.

**2** Bring the elderflowers home and get your other ingredients ready before starting to make the cordial. Don't forget to wash your hands!

**3** With the help of an adult, slice two lemons. Add them to a pot of water with your elderflowers and around four tablespoons of citric acid (you should be able to buy citric acid at world food stores or pharmacies).

**4** Bring the mixture to the boil.

**5** When it has reached boiling point, remove the pot from the heat and drape a tablecloth over the top of it. Leave the mixture to infuse overnight.

**6** Strain the liquid through a fine sieve into another pot and add around 800 g of white sugar.

**7** Bring the mixture back to the boil, stirring frequently so the sugar starts to dissolve.

**8** Simmer for five minutes.

**9** With the help of an adult, pour the cordial into clean, glass bottles while the liquid is still warm. This ensures the lid of the bottle will seal as the liquid cools and keeps it fresher for longer.

**10** Serve your homemade cordial to friends and enjoy a cool drink at a picnic in the countryside.

# 40

# Catch butterflies with a net

Catching butterflies in a net lets you see them up close. However, butterflies are fragile and have delicate wings, so you need to be very careful. The best time to search for butterflies is during the day when temperatures are at their highest.

## You'll need:

butterfly net, notepad and pen, camera

## What to do:

**1** With the help of an adult, buy a suitable net to catch butterflies.

**2** Practise using your net. Use slow, controlled movements and place the centre of the net over your target.

**3** When you have caught a butterfly, hold your net steady in one hand. With the other hand, gently hold the netting so the butterfly can't escape. Look at the details of the butterfly, especially its wings. If you can't identify the species, take a picture or remember how it looks.

**4** Release your hold on the net. Then use the palm of your hand to push the bottom of the net and butterfly to the opening.

**5** Allow the butterfly to fly away on its own.

# Can you catch and identify these butterflies?

**Common blue**

⭐ **15** POINTS

**Orange tip**

⭐ **25** POINTS

**Red admiral**

⚪ **5** POINTS

**Painted lady**

⚪ **5** POINTS

**Large skipper**

⭐ **30** POINTS

**Speckled wood**

⭐ **40** POINTS

**TOP SPOT!**

Score 30 eco points for finding out how to help save butterflies and moths. Visit the Butterfly Conservation website to learn more.

**30** ECO POINTS

# 41

# See a hare boxing

Hares are beautiful creatures that are wonderful to see. If you are lucky, you might see a hare boxing. Boxing takes place in March during breeding season between two adult hares. When the female hare has had enough of her potential suitor, she faces him in a 'boxing match', rearing up on her hind legs and jabbing him with her front.

## You'll need:

binoculars, camera

## What to do:

**1** To have the best chance of spotting boxing hares, explore wooded areas or open fields during March.

**2** Look out for long brown ears peeking through grass, as this is often the first thing you see if a hare is close by.

**3** If you spot a hare in March, try to follow their movements. It could be a male on the trail of a female.

**4** Always keep your distance so that you don't disturb the hares.

**5** If you are using a camera, remember to turn the flash off.

How many of these things can you spot?

## A hare running

**25 POINTS**

Hares can reach speeds of up to 72 km per hour and often run in a zigzag pattern.

## Leveret

**30 POINTS**

A leveret is a young hare. The mother will have 3–4 litters of 2–4 young each year. They are born above ground and are extremely vulnerable.

## Boxing hares

**35 POINTS**

Score 30 eco points for reporting any sightings of brown hares to The Hare Preservation Trust.

**30 ECO POINTS**

# 42

# Learn birdsong

Birds call to attract mates, defend their territory and just for the joy of singing! A great time to learn birdsong is early mornings between March and July when birds are most vocal.

## You'll need:

notepad and pen, recording device

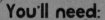

## What to do:

**1** Find a quiet spot under a tree, next to a hedgerow or in an open field.

**2** Close your eyes and listen. When you hear a bird calling, open your eyes and write down the species of bird if you know it. Describe the call or use a device to record it. This means you can listen back to the call whenever you want.

**3** If you don't know the species of bird, describe its features so that you can identify it later.

**4** Try not to learn more than 3–5 bird calls at once, so you don't become overwhelmed. When you feel confident with those, learn another 3–5 calls. In no time at all you will be able to identify a species of bird just by hearing its song.

Here are some common birds and a description of their calls to help you get started. Put a tick against each species when you see and hear them in the wild.

### House sparrow

Listen for a short, high-pitched series of chirps and cheeps. You might hear sparrows chattering to one another.

**10 POINTS**

### Robin

Robins are often the first birds you'll hear in the morning. Listen for long whistles broken by pauses.

**10 POINTS**

### Woodpigeon

A woodpigeon has a low call made up of five-note phrases that are often repeated.

**10 POINTS**

### Wren

This tiny bird can call more than 100 notes in just a few seconds. Listen for a loud, superfast, high-pitched outburst.

**30 POINTS**

# 43

# Spot different breeds of sheep

There are many different breeds of sheep in the countryside. Sheep are bred for their appearance, for milk and for their meat.

**You'll need:**

walking boots, binoculars

## What to do:

**1** When you are next in the countryside, see if you can spot these different breeds of sheep. Use the binoculars to pinpoint the different features of the sheep.

**2** Keep your distance from sheep, especially if they have lambs with them.

**3** You might notice a patch of colour on the sheep – farmers add this so that they can identify who the sheep belong to.

Suffolk
**15** POINTS

Hebridean
**25** POINTS

Bluefaced Leicester
**20** POINTS

Jacob
**40** POINTS

TOP SPOT!

While you are looking for sheep, can you spot these creatures in the fields?

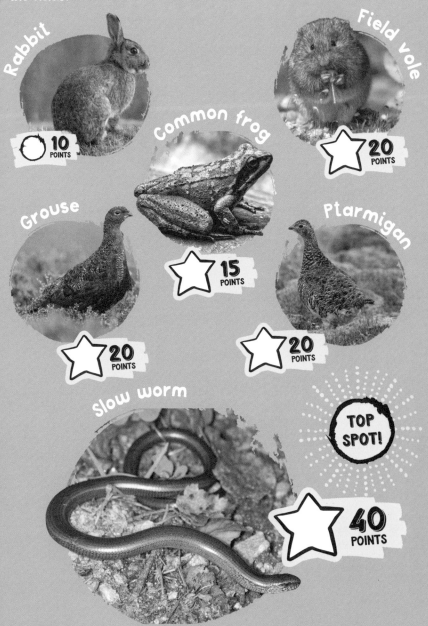

Rabbit

10 POINTS

Field vole

20 POINTS

Common frog

15 POINTS

Grouse

20 POINTS

Ptarmigan

20 POINTS

Slow worm

TOP SPOT!

40 POINTS

# 44

# Go camping

Camping is a great way to experience the outdoors and make precious memories.

Ask an adult to help you research areas near you to camp. Investigate the laws on wild camping in the UK. General rules include seeking permission from the landowner to camp, being respectful of people and wildlife around you, and leaving no trace you were there.

## You'll need:

tent, sleeping bag, notepad and pen, cooking equipment, prepared food, plates and cutlery

## What to do:

**1** Practise pitching your tent in your garden or a park, so you know you have all your equipment and nothing is broken.

**2** Write a list of all the camping gear you need and tick it off as you pack – you don't want to forget something vital!

**3** Prepare and pack food that can be eaten cold or is easy to heat up.

**4** Make sure you camp near to public toilets, or make other arrangements beforehand.

Score 30 eco points for clearing up before you go home – leave no trace that you stayed in the countryside.

**30** ECO POINTS

How many of these things can you spot when you're camping?

## Camping chair

**10** POINTS

## Blanket

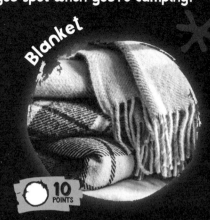

**10** POINTS

## Campfire

**10** POINTS

## Marshmallows

**10** POINTS

## Flask

**10** POINTS

## Torch

**10** POINTS

# 45

# Stargaze

The countryside is the perfect place to get a clear view of the night sky without the light pollution you find in the city.

## You'll need:

blanket, flask, binoculars/telescope, smartphone

## What to do:

**1** Pack a flask to keep you warm while you stargaze.

**2** With help from an adult, find an open area of the countryside with an unobstructed view of the sky. Then lie on a blanket looking upwards. Use binoculars/a telescope to get a clearer view of the night sky.

**3** Use an app like Star Chart on a smartphone to learn more about the constellations and planets, simply by holding the phone up to the sky.

**4** On a clear night, the moon should be quite easy to spot. On the night of your stargaze, what phase of the moon can you see?

**5** Look outwards from the moon – what else can you see in the night sky? Planets look like vibrant stars and it's possible to spot Mercury, Venus, Mars, Jupiter and Saturn with the naked eye throughout the year.

There is so much to see in the sky at night-time, it may seem a little overwhelming. Start by trying to spot these star patterns and constellations.

The Big Dipper

**15** POINTS

The Little Dipper

**15** POINTS

Orion

**20** POINTS

**30** POINTS

Taurus

Gemini

TOP SPOT!

**40** POINTS

# 46

# Go badger watching

It can be difficult to track down a badger on your own. They have very good hearing and an impressive sense of smell.

## You'll need:

internet access, warm clothing, torch

## What to do:

**1** With an adult, search the internet for local badger groups to join for an evening of badger watching, for example The Badger Trust.

**2** The best months to watch badgers are June and July when the cubs play above ground. Badgers become less active in the winter.

**3** Wear warm, dark clothing and a hat and gloves to go badger watching, both to keep warm and to cover up as much of your scent as possible. Bring a torch, but never shine it directly on a badger.

**4** Arrive in plenty of time and always listen to the advice of the group leader.

**5** Never try to feed badgers. Your aim is to watch the badgers and learn, but not disturb them.

**6** Be patient – it will be worth the wait to see badgers so close to you!

When you are badger watching, see if you can spot...

Badger sett entrance

Badger pawprint

**15** POINTS

**15** POINTS

Badger fur

**20** POINTS

Badger

And hopefully you'll
see a badger!

**30** POINTS

# 47

# Go on a glow worm walk

Glow worms are actually small beetles. They spend most of their life (up to three years) as larvae, feeding on snails and living under rocks or in long grass. When they mature during summer, the adults only live for a few weeks to mate.

Females light up to attract a male, giving out a fantastic glow that shines brightly in the dark.

## You'll need:

internet access, sturdy shoes

## What to do:

**1** With help from an adult, visit The Wildlife Trusts website to find the best nature reserve to spot glow worms. They are rare in Scotland, but found across England and Wales.

**2** Plan a visit around early July when the adults emerge from their larval stage.

**3** The best time to head out on a glow worm walk is a dry, warm evening. Let your eyes adjust to the dark and leave your torch at home – you'll be more likely to spot the glow of a flightless female in stalks of tall grass.

When you go on a glow worm walk, keep your eyes peeled for other insects that are active after the sun goes down.

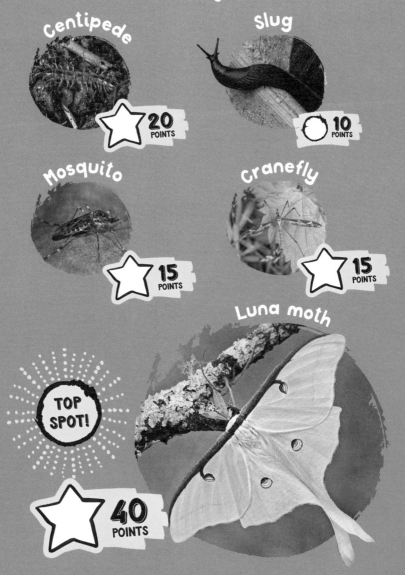

### Centipede
20 POINTS

### Slug
10 POINTS

### Mosquito
15 POINTS

### Cranefly
15 POINTS

### Luna moth

TOP SPOT!

40 POINTS

Did you know that glow worms give out light by a chemical reaction in their bodies which involves an enzyme, a molecule called luciferin, and oxygen? The result is a glow that ranges from blue to green.

# Write a nature poem

Get creative and write a poem about your favourite location or memory of the countryside.

## You'll need:

notebook and pen

## What to do:

1. Start by writing down words, phrases or descriptions of your favourite countryside memories, so you have a bank of content to pull from when putting your poem together.

2. Poems don't need to rhyme! Just write down your thoughts and try to find a natural rhythm. Your poem can be as long or as short as you like.

3. Line breaks let the reader know when to pause, so use them regularly to help with the flow of your poem.

4. Poems usually make people feel some kind of emotion, so try adding a personal touch. For instance, include how you felt or what you could smell.

5. Once you are happy with your poem, why not read it out loud to family or friends in your favourite countryside spot?

# Do a nature sketch

One way to improve your focus and observational skills is to do a nature sketch.

## You'll need:

paper, pencils

## What to do:

1. Choose a favourite spot in the countryside. Take a moment to decide what you want to draw.

2. You can either sketch the view or focus on one thing like a single flower.

3. Start by lightly sketching the main shapes. Once you are happy that everything fits on the paper, add in lots of detail, shading and colour.

4. You could go back to the same spot once every few months and draw the same thing. How do the drawings compare during the different seasons?

Score 10 eco points for using recycled paper to draw with.

10
ECO
POINTS

# Go to a farmers' market

Buying produce at a farmers' market is an easy way to eat locally grown, sustainable, fresh food. It's also an opportunity to ask where your food comes from and how it is produced.

## You'll need:

money, your own bags

## What to do:

**1** With an adult, research the different foods that grow throughout the year. If you have some knowledge of seasonal produce, you'll know what to expect at the market and be able to think about what you want to buy.

**2** Plan what time of day to visit the market – going early means you will have the best selection to choose from. Going later in the day may mean you get the best deals.

**3** Take a risk and try a new food you have never tasted before. Learn how to cook a meal with the ingredient.

**4** Have fun looking at all the colourful stalls!

See if you can spot these items when you go to a farmers' market.

Seasonal fruit and vegetables

10 POINTS

Eggs

5 POINTS

Cheese

Cakes

10 POINTS

10 POINTS

Jams and chutney

Fresh flowers

15 POINTS

20 POINTS

Score 30 eco points for buying produce from a farmers' market. Remember that by selling locally, the farmers are minimising the waste and pollution they create.

30 ECO POINTS

# Index

# Take on the other i-SPY challenges!

Discover more fun and fascinating
i-SPY books at collins.co.uk/i-SPY